CROSSING THE BLUE LINE

As well as previously uncollected poems,
Crossing the Blue Line also includes work from the following
collections:
Come Sun, Come Snow (2000) published by Bradshaw Books
and *Aherlow* (2004) published by Rectory Press.

ISBNs
PARENT: 978-1-78237-271-4
EPUB: 978-1-78237-272-1
MOBI: 978-1-78237-273-8
PDF: 978-1-78237-274-5

A CIP catalogue for this book is available from the National Library.
Published by ORIGINAL WRITING LTD., Dublin, 2013.
Printed by CLONDALKIN GROUP, Glasnevin, Dublin 11

CROSSING THE BLUE LINE

New and selected poems

Dympna Dreyer

ORIGINAL WRITING

for Del

Acknowledgements

Acknowledgments and thanks are due to the editors of the following, in which some of the new poems in this volume first appeared: Figments, Oxford Magazine, Poetry Ireland Review, Southword, Stroan, The Church Mouse, The Moth, The SHop. Waterford Review, Women's Work.

My sincere thanks to Mark Roper without whose help and encouragement my poems would never have seen the light of day. Thanks also to Edward Power and to the publishers of Crossing the Blue Line - Original Writing.

To Eileen Dreyer, (wise as always) who advised me to take this course.

Contents

Interlude

2

3

4

5

Overture

A chapel of branches in a grove
A candle on the hundred altars of a sycamore
A congregation of birds bristling at dawn

A cuckoo love-longing
A creation without pain
A child fostered by sun

A day-bright child
A dancer by moonlight
A daisy with open eyes

An exercise book blotted with tears
An echoing cane
An eggshell where cracks begin to appear

A full voice chanting Latin in the high stalls
A fleeting moment of transcendence
A fragmented rosary

A green light changing quickly
A grinding crash a burning smell
A grave of buried memory

A glorious ride on a carousel
A galaxy of nights in the Bois de Boulogne
A gold pin rusting in the hem of a wedding dress

A hint of blue sky between darkening trees
A heightened promise of a fruitful garden
A hymn to two budding flowers

A haunting autumn
A hundred years of pain
A happy sun smiling again

A little woman curled and withered
A mad mirror
A muddled house that time deserted

A pen always in doubt
A past trying to catch up with itself
A train carriage put out to grass

A wax wreath whitening on a family grave
A watch slipping on a shrunken wrist
A young smile on an old woman's face

1

A Torn out Page

Made stand on her desk.
A torn out page
of childish scrawls

pinned to her back.
Sound of a bell.
Sniggering classmates filter out.

"Disgraceful work!"
Piggy eyes
wet bulldog mouth.

The sharp cane falls.

Every new page a challenge now,
her black pen trawls

and digs and hesitates
and cuts.
Always in doubt.

What did she write about
that little girl of long ago:
what did she write?

Aherlow

Once there was this:
a child, her father's hand
a clanking bucket
tall dark tree on the horizon.

She doesn't remember if they ever reached the well.

She returns one autumn evening
driving through mist
to a house of drawn blinds,
parks her car in mud and silence
at the yard gate leading to the farm.

Stretching before her one long field all the way to the horizon.

Surely there were two fields
and beyond the top field
tall, tall trees.

Light has come on in the porch
a door opens
the yard's alive with shadows.

She doesn't remember if they ever reached the well.

Oscar the Bad Rabbit

Mama says you're really sick.
No school to-day.
You sit in Dada's big chair beside the range.

Mama is baking scones.
She has filled the space over the oven with torytops.
You can smell their piney smell, hear them frizzle.

You must drink lots.
The red lemonade is full of bubbles that tickle your nose.
It tastes much nicer than at Christmas.

You've a new book called Oscar the Bad Rabbit.
You've wanted it for ages and ages.
Ever since Dada bought you The King of the Bunnies.

There are bunnies in the well field.
They run when we clatter the bucket.
You wish the well was full of lemonade.

Mama has come in from the line.
She snuggles the blanket tighter around you.
You are my little rabbit.

You're glad Mike is at school.
You can never read when he's around.
Once he tore the cover off your very favourite book.

Mama has turned on the wireless.
Missesdalesdiary, she says.
She gives you another glass of lemonade.

The ashes are grey and red when they fall into the ash box.
And then they turn all grey.
It's as well you're good or you'd go to hell .

You wonder who cuts down the trees for the devil's big fire
When you're big you'll help Dada with the crosscut.
Won't let it wobble like Mike does.

Oscar the Bad Rabbit always gets his sums wrong.
There's a picture of him at the blackboard on Page 6.
Ages ago you got a lollipop from Miss Mac for getting your
        sums right.

Oh, spilled lemonade on the cover.
Only a little drop.
There, wiped it off with the end of your nightie.

Mama says you'll have to go to bed for a little nap.
You never go to bed during the day now that you're in school.
But Mama says just this once you can bring your book to bed.

Mary's hotwater bottle makes a big bump in your bed.
You kick it with your toes and it makes a wobbly
    tummy-rumble sound.
Teddy, sit up there on the pillow and listen to me read.

First Flight

Dada painted the walls my favourite blue.
All night the whirr of Mama's sewing machine.
The curtains had a lacy frill on top
And tie-backs that hung on golden hooks.

I brought all my books from Mama's room.
They fitted nicely on the wardrobe shelf.
The prayerbook Nana gave me pushed to the back –
That sad lady on the cover
A million spears going through her heart.

Mama read two stories right through
Instead of just her usual one.
Before she blew the candle out
She gave me an extra hug.

I had to hold Teddy tight.
He wasn't used to the big bed
And might have fallen out.
I told him the bats couldn't get in.
Mama had checked the window twice.

I woke to wood pigeons calling
From the tall trees in the grove
Right under my window –
Only them and me.

The lino smelled of turpentine
Was sticky under my bare feet
As I looped the trembling curtains
Back on their golden hooks.

Infelice

Mama is lighting the Aladdin lamp.
The mantle glows blue.
The globe is a tall hat.
She pulls her chair near the lamp.

Her hair turns blue. Her blouse turns blue.
There is a picture of a lady in a red lacy dress
on the cover of her book.
Mama's hands are quiet. Her eyes are quiet.

I lie on the sofa with my cat, Derek.
We spell out the letters
on the cover of the book -
Infelice

Mama, I can read all the letters on your book!
She looks at me from far away.
Her eyes don't know me.
The mantle turns from blue to white.

Summer

tea in the garden
the wind-up gramophone
Panis Angelicus
china cups ring vibrato
Russells' tractor passing the gate

The Garden

A blue day.
My new crepesoles
A scummy green.
Dada pushing the mowing machine.
Mama and me cleaning the weeds.

Snip snap snip snap!
A foxglove with a pointy cap.
A silk red pompom
Tickling my feet.
That's a poppy love - see-
Its bold black eye winks up at me.

Mary there, her cardboard box pram.
Belinda sleeping inside.
Poking my finger into one closed eye.
Click a poppy black leer.
Screams scream in my ear -
Boodeyman, Boodeyman

Whorts

Leaving the old coach road behind
We entered a greenlit world of furze and heather
On the foothills of Slieve na Muc.
Our legs and thighs scratched through summer frocks.
The sun glinted on our empty cans
Made them almost too hot to handle.
There was a multitude of whisperings
Bees, gnats, smaller unseen things.
And somewhere the suggestion of a stream.

Ber's shout - I saw them first!
The ping of berries on tin.
There's more. There's more.
I tore painfully through furze
and there they were.
Hundreds of black-eyed whorts winking
From their green nests, begging to be picked.
I dropped the can
Crammed fistfuls of sweetness into my mouth.
Ber took one look, whooped
And ran about in circles shouting
My sister's a Red Indian.

Let's find that stream.
We followed the inviting whisper deep into the wood
Where trees grew thickly dark
And wet loam squelched our sandalled feet.
The sun had disappeared.
Ber held her nose.
Hundreds of shiny-black flies
Whorts on the wing
Circled, buzzed around a bolster
Striped grey and white
Like the one on Nana's bed.
Come away from there, Ber yelled,
Slapping flies from her face.
Inching a step nearer
I saw two eyeless sockets teeming with life.
The badger was very dead.

Mama tumbled the two half-cans
Into an enamel bowl.
You could hardly see the whorts
For leaves and brambly bits.
But when they were strained and washed
And she'd added the top of the milk
There was enough to fill four saucers.
I squashed mine with the back of a spoon
Squirting their inky insides into the milk.
Watching it turn from grimy grey- white
To wash-day blue.

Making Jam

Eye-watering bite of cloves
Skim-dip of wooden spoon
Red sticky footprints on stone.

A cold saucer testing
Scalded jars resting
Strained muslin
Bandaging upturned chair.

Small green envelope
Flutters to the floor
Wooden spoon sinking
Someone quietly closes the door.

Mama, the pan is boiling over
Mama, there's red stuff all over the range
Mama, Paul the postman came.

Harvest at Russells

Hot-buttered honeyed days.
Bastable bread and sweet-canned tea
in the cornfield.

Sliding down ricks,
stubble pricks through summer frocks.
Hands sweat corn at barn dance.

The Game

Scurrying like mice
up the stairs. Long nighties
tucked around our toes.
We peeped between bannisters.

Reverent hush. Green light
of the wireless warms up.
Red-faced neighbours, cloth caps -
firelight shadows on the ceiling.

Ber said it was Fionn
and his men hunting deer.
I saw Setanta.
I saw the hound of Culann.

Lisvernane

grey powder mixed with water iodine smell
veined hands of master pouring in
white china wells flow over
smear black
brass plates click
nibs scrape
ink -
blot

haiku

first communicants
white pneumonia dresses
snow flurries in May

Mary Mary

The Hail Mary seemed easy at first.
I'd a big sister called Mary
and grace was a familiar word.

When the wheels screeched on the pig-cart
I'll grace the axle, Boss.
I hated that black, smelly stuff.

Mary full of grace was a puzzle
but maybe being the oldest like Nana
she'd started to stiffenup.

The fruit of thywomb was what stumped me.
No thywomb tree grew in our orchard.
Just apples, pears, the usual stuff.

Mama was no help at all.
Her voice sounded kind of choking
That's religion, love.

Dad left down his paper.
When we talk to people in Heaven
we use their special words.

So thywomb trees grew in Heaven.
God had a haggard like ours.
Did his mama make jam and tarts.

Did the angels squabble like us -
who'll be the first to fill the basket -
Did God say that's enough.

We do! We do!

The gallery was scarey. We sat in the front row - Mama, Miss
Mac and me. So I can see how the children behave, Miss Mac
whispered to Mama.

My head barely came to the top of the kneeler. A huge noth-
ingness below me. I held Mama's hand tight. *Do you renounce the
devil with all his works and pomps? We do! We do! Do you renounce
the vanities of this wicked world? We do! We do!*

Suddenly Miss Mac's face went red - Oh my God, I forgot!
She fiddled in her huge handbag, then shoved a pair of horn rimmed
glasses on her fat nose. They made her look cross and mean. Grab-
bing her brown leather missal from the pew in front of her she tore out
a page from the back and scribbled like mad. Tearing a page out
of her missal! I know what my Dada said when I tore a page out
of *The Life of the Little Flower.*

Go now and give that to your Dada. There's a good girl. Quick
now! Blowing on the ink for a couple of seconds she folded the
page and handed it to me. Mama frowned and whispered - She's
far too young. Wouldn't know what to do. I thought Miss Mac
would burst as her face went even redder and her eyes popped -
Nonsense, she'll be going to school next year.

The steps down were full of holes and went round and round
and round forever. The heels of my new black patent shoes could get
stuck. Clang hum Clang hum rang the iron steps like Dada's tuning fork
when he struck it off the table. Down down, round and round.

I would never get to the bottom! Suddenly, around a bend I saw through the steps little bits of coloured tiles like in the porch at home. Then, I was down facing the miles and miles of floor to the altar.

My shoes made a lovely happy tapping noise on the tiles, the sound the Friar Burke made when he nailed a horsehoe on to the half door of Billy's stable. My toes hurt a little and when I wriggled them the leather gave a little squeak. Tap squeak. Tap squeak.

Halfway up the aisle I saw Lily Maloney the postmistress in a red costume and a black lacey doyley on her head. I had never seen her out of her shop coat before. Across the aisle our nextdoorneighbour Mickie Russell knelt on his cap on one knee. His eyes were closed and he was making a funny noise through his nose.

I could see the bishop now in his long dress and magic cloak up high on the altar. He was going hammer and tongs, his wizard's hat shaking and dipping as he raised or lowered his fist … *demon drink … flying in the face of God…*I knew God was locked up behind that little gold door on the altar. How could a demon fly in his face?

A man with a bald head and creaking boots had come out of nowhere carrying a wooden box on a long handle. People were putting money into the box.

Suddenly I saw Dada looking round from where he knelt beside his 6ᵗʰ class boys, all grown up in their long trousers. I ran all the rest of the way till I reached him. He put his arms around me. You're a great big brave girl, he whispered when he read the note. Now go quietly and sit with your sister till the ceremony is over. *Do you solemnly pledge not to drink alcohol until you are eighteen years of age. We do! We do !*

Ber sat on the other side of the aisle. I squeezed in past the long rustling white dresses. Sit back there and don't move or make a sound -

It was the first time I'd seen Ber look serious .She was the madcap of the family... here, mind my beads for me. *My dear boys and girls, the time has come for you to approach the altar of God and be anointed with the oil of chrism so that you can henceforth walk without fear as soldiers of Christ.*

Now is The Time, screamed the school choir. I sat back in my seat and took Ber's white rosary out of its purse. Swinging my feet up and down in the now empty pew, I watched the sparkling beads being mirrored in my shiny new black patent shoes.

Shepherd

Ours was the front pew in one of the side aisles
in the village church.
We sat in order of seniority
Dad on the outside
me penned-in on the inner edge
under the painted smile of St. Teresa.
I was always afraid she would topple over
as the seat shook from our giggles
at familiar faces on the other side.

Once an old priest tripped going down
the altar steps
dropping the ciborium
scattering the Communion breads.
We watched in horror
as a mountainy man
jumped from his seat on the other aisle
clearing the altar rails like a sheep over a stone wall
shovelling the small white discs into the ciborium
with big hands more used
to throwing fodder into a stall

Spoiled

Faded red and green decorations
concertina'd smokey walls,
matched verdigris of frayed soutane,
livid face of man
who sat alone
in the far corner of Kiely's pub.

Soft white hands raised a shaking glass
in our direction.
Happy Christmas, Missus.
And you too -
Mama's voice was strange.

Stop staring, pet
Drink up your lemonade.
Leaving her sherry untouched
she pushed me to the door.
What was it your father said he wanted?

How was the big day in town.
I suppose you're stuffed
with lemonade and biscuits.
Dada, she didn't let me finish my lemonade.
The spoiled priest was there,
Mama whispered.

The Gate

Our dark valley
Walled in by hills, want
The consumption

The protestant
Creamery manager
Hanged in a barn

The swollen body
Of a farmer's daughter
In O'Briens pond

My father
Elbows
On Russells gate

Looking up
At the world
Calling me

An aeroplane shines
Overhead
Flock of wild geese

The New Look

Later that day we crossed over the street from the Nursing Home - "to buy mourning", my mother whispered.

We had been in D. Murphy & Sons, Drapers before when Auntie Maggie married "beneath her". Even Ber who knew almost everything hadn't been able to figure that one out.

The shop was huge and dark and this time there was a lady sitting high up in a glass cage very near the ceiling almost like the lady in the circus. I kept waiting for her to fly out the little window and down. Instead a train thing clicked up to her window and gave her money and then clicked back again.

There were oohs and aahs and "sorry for your trouble". Black suits and coats appeared, disappeared into a closet with my mother. Finally she came out wearing a long black coat down to her toes and what looked like the roman helmet on page 3 of our history book pulled down over her head.

"Oh, there you are... this is *it*... oh really ...perfect. We have just got in The New Look from Dublin - Im *sure* you've heard of it - down to your toes - and you do carry it so well with your slim waist - oh you must agree! Walk over there to the long mirror near the door. Plenty of light there."

Ber looked at me and back at Mama. We tried till our faces were purple and our eyes bulged but we couldn't keep in the laughing.

"Get outside that door till I'm finished. Disgracing me on a day like this in front of the whole of Tipperary town!"

It was bucketing outside but I didn't feel the rain on my new pink bow and my crepesoled sandals.

"I didn't know he was going to die"
Tears and snots distorted Ber's small face.

"Poor Mama" I howled "what are we all going to do".

Upstairs

When we got back to the empty house
friends and relations gone their separate ways,
we sat in the cold parlour, tired, numb
having nothing to say to each other.
A thump in his room overhead.
A shoe hitting the floor. Then another.
Always our cue that he was getting into bed
when we would switch the wireless
from the measured tones of Síle Ní Bhriain
to Pete Murray on Luxembourg.

Our eyes said to each other:
You go. You go.
That time we threw cushions in the parlour
smashing the vase our parents got as a wedding gift
when someone had to go and tell our mother.
Finally my brother rose
holding on to the bannisters
as he climbed the stairs
like an old man out of breath.

Which of us let him in?
Shep lying there on the bed.
Couldn't get him to move.
Someone must have left a pair of Dad's shoes.
We cried then
holding on to each other.
Even my brother, so grown up.
Even my brother.

Everyone knew

Josie McCarthy from back the road
hadn't a chance
was wild as a goat.
When she rode her High-Nellie
to Riversdale
for the late-night dance
she'd stop half way,
dump her corset behind a ditch.
She married a rich farmer
from somewhere near Bruff.
Owned a fur coat
and a wall-to-wall rug.

Mick Neale was sure
to turn out bad.
Considered himself
a bit of a lad.
Slinged from school
more often than not.
Had brilliantined hair
and a red knotted scarf.
Stole a pellet gun for a dare.
Took potshots at the neighbours' cats.
Joined the Brothers
never looked back.

Mrs Fahy from Ballinacourty
a poor widow-woman
no one to support her.
For half a crown and a bowl of dripping
she washed the neighbours' dirty linen.
Wore a shawl and a beaming smile
as her swollen feet
took her many a mile
to find a day's work
in whatever direction.
Had to pay five bob
to the church collection.

Everyone longed
for Mick the Postman's knock.
A parcel from Boston,
letter from New York.
Around Christmas time
he was never sober.
A drink at each stop
Glencush to Gurtavoher.
Christmas cards got very short shrift
tossed from his bag over Stonepark Bridge.
Express Delivery via the waters below
floating out on the tide of the Aherlow.

Mary Maloney from Bansha way
was a pure saint
told her beads night and day.
When Redemptorists came
for the village mission
we shook in our shoes
in abject contrition.
She's a model, they said
for Irish mothers.
Thirteen children
expecting another.
When she ran off with the hired man
everyone said they knew all along.

The Friar, Cotter and Johnny Denn

The Friar, Cotter and Johnny Denn
Lived near the Galtee Mountains.
The Friar and Cotter, odd-job men.
Johnny worked for the Council.

Their cottage was a two-roomed shack.
A hole in the roof for a chimney.
The walls were neither white nor black.
A grey rag flapped at the window.

The Friar worked on local farms
Milking and fencing ditches.
An old corn sack to keep him warm.
A rope held up his britches.

Cotter journeyed from field to field
Helped harvest the corn and hay.
Spuds-in-dripping his only meal
When the cocks came home on the dray.

Johnny was weathered from sleet and rain
As he steamrolled grit and tar.
Loved black tea from his old billy can.
The odd packet of Woodbines, a jar.

The Friar, Cotter and Johnny Denn
Three brothers now under the sod.
Slaved all their lives for other men.
Everyone knew 'twas the will of God.

For one and all

For Mrs. Davy on wash day, water into blue wine
Wind-charger flailing like the hommers o' hell
Spring well touched by a green god
Light and shade of old trees in the glen.

For cooing woodpigeons, cock-pheasant's squawk
Carbolic soap in icy morning gasp
Reading by candlelight in forbidden hours
Rag doll Molly's comforting clasp.

For the Friar Bourke hoisting churns on cart
Hip bath beside the range, scorching towels
Tinkers on roadside mullocking pots and pans
Rescuing eggs from sceachs, hens laying out.

For Jack-is-alive and pictures in the fire
Scalding stew and spicy apple tart
Míle murder, vase in smithereens
Singsongs around the piano after dark.

For Tom Coffey's forge, stink of burning hooves
Dry-mouthed sloes, red-lipsticked haws
Fiddle-faced women fasting to Sunday Mass
Hay for the reindeers, cake for Santa Claus.

For wellies crunching nicely in the snow
Dada foostering his pipe, Mama reading
Lying in the meadow giving shapes to clouds
Prickly holly chain, thread and bodkin needle.

For Mike jig-acting during the rosary
Ruaille buaille at sports in Lisvernane
Breakfast of soda bread and googy egg
Mick Russell swiping at feocadáns.

For Patrick's serpent locked in Lake Diheen
Hallowe'en shanachus, April Fool
Playing house with chaneys, hours on hours
Packing trunk for boarding school.

Daisies

Mama and me picking daisies
carefully one by one.
Long stems intact
one looped into the other.
Around my neck
a perfect chain.

Together circling time
on a cardboard clock.
Pushing a cardboard mouse
round and round:
The big hand is at twelve.
The little one tells the hour.

How old time has become.

The Snow Queen

Last child left at home,
her siblings gone to boarding school.
Big house
lost among fields and trees.

Last child alive in the world.
Fills the empty spaces in her cobby house
with images from fairy tales,
her house guarded by
the snow queen
who has pierced
her heart.

Last child alive in the world.
No longer fears being alone,
has forgotten the bad dream.
Swings from a looped-up rope
in the grove
or listens to her songs
echoing
in the well field.

All her life she has looked up at a snowy peak.
All her life has known
this was her very own mountain.
White and safe and clean.

Interlude

This book -
Practical Meditations.
Brown leather cover,
hand-stitched edges.
'To the use of'
faintly pencilled
on the fly leaf.

They let me keep it
with the white notepaper,
the ornate workboxes,
given to me
by well wishers
when I joined the convent
at eighteen.

Heavy smell of incense,
pure voices chanting Latin
in the high stalls,
common moment of transcendence.
Holy pictures pasted
over personal mirrors -
no reflection of self
to remain.

But the personal intruded-
communal confession,
recital of faults,
petty jealousies.
Disillusioned,
I left.

My mother ashamed,
wanting to wipe out
the memory of my failure,
destroyed all the pictures
of me veiled, long skirted
taken on her first visit.
My daughter, the nun!

2

The Drawer

Your card lies still in the chiffonier.
Ma chère...à la recherché de temps passé.
A Paris skyline once streaked with tears.

That drawer unopened for many years.
A fit of cleaning-out the other day.
Your card lies still in the chiffonier.

Ma chère... is that an inkblot or a tear?
I turn it over. How the picture fades.
A Paris skyline once streaked with tears.

Red mini-skirt, pillbox hat, sixties gear.
Seeds from a broken lavender bouquet.
Your card lies still in the chiffonier.

*Ma chère...*how many days, how many years
Have these old memories been locked away.
A Paris skyline once streaked with tears.

The drawer sticks. I soap it till it clears.
Freed now I can open it any day.
Your card lies still in the chiffonier.
A Paris skyline once streaked with tears

Carousel

He wore flared trousers
Jesus sandals
an open-neck shirt.

She wore a blue shirtwaister
buttoned to the neck
stiletto heels that hurt.

He took his coffee strong
with a dash of cognac -
liked to act tough.

She loved ice-cream
hot chocolate in a bowl
sweet songs of love.

His broken English
her elementary French.
Only love could tell.

That summer in the Bois.
Two crazy children
riding on a carousel.

haiku 2

He hands me a peach
I taste his love's sweetness
Within me an orchard

Ritual

Shutters rattle open in the boulangerie.
Grandmère surveys the early morning street.
Papa, she yells down the lift well
In the blue-tiled floor.
Quick, Papa, quick… a fresh baguette
Your crispiest croissants, a crusty battard.
Père Alfonse approaches our boulevard.
Early Mass is over… hurry, Papa, hurry".
My god why is he so slow!

Grandpère shovels long bread into baskets
Fiercely bangs the furnace door.
The lift cuts into place
In the upper floor.
Martyred in the flaming colours
Of the furnace glare
The old man chants his every morning prayer -
Let him eat cake, the fat Abbé.
Let him eat cake!

1968 and all that

Dirty Communist, Grandmère shrieks
As the young assistant baker
Lays out twelve charred black offerings
Coffined in long baskets
On the tiled boulangerie floor.

Give us this day our daily bread
The bold red lettering
On the stained-glass panel
Bloodies his white-coated exit
Through the swing doors.

Don't just stand there, Papa.
Hurry, hurry, hurry.
Do something, can't you.
Send for the Abbé.
Call the CRS.

Grandpère shrugs
As he buries in the dustbin
The spoiled batch of baguettes.
If you want to make the omelette, Maman
You have to break some eggs.

Smokescreen

Sometimes when he first went away
she'd take an old jacket he'd left behind
hug it to her for a little while.
It smelled of Gauloises -
he smoked forty a day.
This was when she could still cry.
Could remember why.

It was only
when she became resigned
senses dimmed
nothing to remind her of him,
that she started to smoke -
Sweet Aftons, Weights, Woodbines -
but never Gauloises.

Conversation Piece

We bought two rings at a bargain price
one golden September day in 1962.
It matches your hair, I laughed.
Two whole days to wait.

Convention placed him beside me
 at our daughter's wedding.
Winter had touched his eyes, his hair.
We busied ourselves with food,
chatted to our neighbours.

Suddenly, he set down his glass
and turning towards me
pulled out from his shirt front
a miniature ring
hanging from a gold chain.

I got it cut down, he said.
Cut down to size no doubt, I said.
You never lost it, he said.

Metalman

His fourteen foot image
Straddles the plinth
Arrogantly down facing
A mutinous sea.
Ships steer east of his threshold
Knowing his bay to be shallow,
His rocks treacherous.

There is no life
Higher than him.
Cloistered behind electric fencing
The black necked sheep
Are dumb acolytes
As they bow to grass in an adjoining field.

We both stare upward
Neck muscles straining back
To see those blue blue eyes.
But he never meets our gaze
As seaward he stares.
We do not threaten so do not exist.

Why are you always so scared?
The road is hot and long and hard
After the soft cushioning grass
And he is bored with its tameness.
I could have replied
I had courage once

But life wore it away;
Waves ripping, entering
Lashing with anger,
Emptying me of sunlight.
But meeting the stare
Of his metal man blue, blue eyes

I was silent.

Rooms with a view

Basement flat Holloway Road.
From your pastry chef's clothes
Sweet smells of cinnamon and jam.
Our baby coming.

Apartment house Braintree, Mass.
Raw steaming nappies.
Hot nights on the fire escape.
Our baby coming.

New house Marshfield-by-the sea.
Bitter tang of seaweed
In the turning tide.
Our children crying.

Petit flat Rue de Javel.
Trying to breathe lightly beside you.
Step carefully around you.
Me and our children

Fourth floor old Henrietta Street.
Eccentric furniture, odd smells.
Greyfriars Abbey floodlit.
Me and my children.

The Wedding Gown Speaks

She was a burning tension in my sequinned breasts,
their stitches stretched from long anticipation.
The satin roses below my waist began to droop.

Spiders were unwelcome guests.
Grey cobwebs replaced the white tracery of my neck.
Its ivory sheen faded, yellowed, cracked.

When the bones of my underskirt collapsed
and she screamed *darling why such haste*
her fate was sealed.

I nudged a trailing sleeve near to the candle flame.
I felt no shame undressing her. Then, quietly as snow
I melted back into innocence.

You Win

I have fulfilled
The vow that I made
When we parted.

My life has been
A blank page
Since then.

No intrigues
No secret
Desires.

I banked down
The fires
Inside me.

And now
Old age has come
And found me

A nun
Tight-lipped
Stony hearted.

Too late
To renounce
The promise I made.

Desire has gone.
Now I belong
To you forever

As though
We had never
Parted.

The string

no no no
this is my life
my life freeing itself
unwinding me
away from you

let it run free

my arms
my feet
untying themselves
feeling the rush
of returning blood

let it unwind

fling open the doors
of the room
the house
open the spaces
between the fingers
of your giant hands

let it run free

free as the swing
swinging all alone
in the high grass
free as the kite
held by a thread
in a child's hand

let it unwind enough
to hang by

The Tree

He had cut down the branches
of her tree
pronounced it dead wood
sawed and lopped
leaving only a trunk.

It had been a beautiful tree
fiery red
lighting up the whole garden.
Birds came and sang on it.
Children climbed to its topmost branch.

She couldn't live with its bleakness
so she trained wisteria
around her tree.
It climbed and twined
wreathing cuts
insinuating
into every nook and scar.

Now the tree
was more wisteria.
The wisteria
more tree.

Already

And suddenly
it's winter.
My garden dies back
to the bare bone.

I lay your ghost
gently
among the silver shadows
of the husks.

The night sky
her black-rimmed eyes
irised in star frost,
shows no mercy.

Soon it will snow

3

Move over old woman

My darling daughter
I want to be the path
Beneath your feet
To keep you safe and steady
As you go.

When you reach a mountain hut
My love will be the warmth
That greets you
The fire that heats you
After the snow.

No matter what path you take
My path will join yours,
My love will guide you
When you grow tired
And your footsteps slow.

Always carefree,
Eager for new experience,
I will be the reins
That hold you back
From your too impulsive flow.

Your wondering eyes,
Your dreaming mind,
The miracle of snow
And snow and snow.

Move over old woman
You are blocking her view of the stars.

The Hospital Visit

To-night in my daughter's house
I switch on all the lights
Hear the tall windows shake
To the beat of my heart
Recall the wind on my face.

To-night in my daughter's house
I drain off in the hall
Hang my coat up to dry
Mop the rain from my eyes
Hear an owl's stupid call.

To-night in my daughter's house
I ease open her bedroom door
Lay her duffel bag on the floor
Her soiled clothes in the bin
Let my mind tuck her in.

to-day

heavy whiteness
sheets too big
small wounded face

her eyes meeting mine
her diagnosis
powerfully unspoken

I turn away
distribute clean clothes
on locker shelves

morphine
at her finger tip
allows a whisper

thanks for bringing, mam,
to-morrow
eyelids flickering

along cold corridors
tomorrow
powerfully echoing

Fragments

This morning for the first time
since you got sick
I didn't go to mass
ignored my sister's message
that she had the flu
and would I ring her back
splashed a full watering can
at McGrath's dog
who peed
against my sun -warmed
geranium pot

After lunch I cleared out
your old room
those clothes
you don't wear any more
flung them fast into a charity bag
including the once favoured sweater
you brought back from Nepal
remember how it made you itch
the tantrum you threw
when it shrunk in the wash

Halfway through
peeling spuds for dinner
that cupboard needs scouring
your giant-size mug
the one you adored
that read
COOL
in tall black letters

CRASH

daffodil day

after the phonecall
a while to sink in
ran out the back
threatened rain hadn't come

windy row of white sheets
high jinks hand stands
rogue birds in the pampas
breaking in   breaking into song

joe's radio next door
tulips from Amsterdam
mick the postman's whistle
walking to his van

I'll drive in to town
a slapup lunch
new poetry book, daffs
a super enormous bunch

after the phonecall
eleven minutes past two o'clock
after the phonecall
should I wait should I ring back

Kovalam

I see your face, strain to hear your voice
and bless the being who first invented Skype!
You tell me all is well - it was your choice.
So - you love the Indian food the ripe

chilli, turmeric. Dani, love, is that type
of food good for you? How do you feel?
(The Ayurvedic treatment - all the hype!
God, please God may it have power to heal).

Why, oh why did India have to appeal
to you. Remember that landslide in Nepal!
(Even now when I think of it I feel
A shuddering horror as I recall

the headlines on the Irish Times. Rock Fall
on Annapurna Trail - which site they didn't say.
I had a singing class in the school hall
when you rang me. A truly blessèd day).

I have to go, Mam   (so much I've left to say).
You tell me all is well. It was your choice.
Another hill to climb, another day.
Your face fades on the screen. I lose your voice.

A Rosary for my daughters

Queen of the May
let your flowers cover the earth
your green fields echo
songs of visiting birds

Queen of the Snow
whitewash our black world
from sea to sea
bow down the stiff-necked
branches of trees

Queen of the Wind
sing your plainchant
in the high galleries
your clean stern breath
scattering disease

Queen of the Sea
wake your grey-green eyes
from wild troubled sleep
bring a morning harvest
to fishers if the deep

Queen of the Hills
of streams and flowering heather
make me a child again
to drink your waters
before they ebb for ever

Queen of the Sun
you sink in the sea
without hurt
rise up on a quiet wave
and smile on us

Queen of the night
string your rosary of stars
more lovely than the sun
your sacred moonlight.

Eileen

October 26ᵗʰ 2002

What wedding gift can I bestow.
Only good fairies at your birth.
Through precious years I watched you grow.

Your time is now, my clock runs slow.
Relentless rhythm of turning earth.
What wedding gift can I bestow.

This special day I see that glow
Which once a Christmas gift conferred.
Through precious years I watched you grow.

I tread softly because I know
Careless footsteps crush flowers to earth.
What wedding gift can I bestow.

I must retreat, old ties forgo.
In my happiness for you, no hurt.
Through precious years I watched you grow.

Do I offer you advice? Oh no.
I trust your wisdom, your sense of worth.
What wedding gift can I bestow.
Through precious years I watched you grow.

Antipodes
for Eileen

Little fledgling
You didn't have to fly
To the other side of the world
To find the sun.

You bring summer
 with you
wherever you go.

Why else in your absence
Do I feel
This icy current in my veins,
This winter in my heart.

nocturne

my daughter is playing the piano
she sings better than she plays
candlelight muddles her pure face

around the fire the family
younger daughter reads, son-in-law
crosses words in The Guardian

see, in the mantel mirror
our lopsided Christmas tree.

4

Different Rooms

A dead bird.
Wreaths of nettles.
She must never let him know
what she'd found in the fridge.

That morning at breakfast
the man's voice coming from the radio
You can only do what you can do.
The birds were all dead in the water by the gasworks.

His hands becoming claws as he buttered her bread.
She couldn't swallow the crumbly mess
though she was very hungry indeed.
The girl has shrunk.
Where on earth could the high chair be.
The girl was lost in that big big chair.

In the bathroom mirror the woman's hair had faded.
How do you do? I'm much better thank you.
The old woman in the mirror nodded.
She tried to comb her own hair
but her hands were slow and unresponsive.
'Your hands are the graceful gesture of a bird'.
The birds were all dead in the water by the gasworks.
She was very cold.

Someone had taken away the bedroom chair.
If she went on tiptoe
she just might reach to the top of the wardrobe.
Yes…it was still there behind Mama's hat
where she had hidden it from the man.
It felt warm and comforting around her neck
until she looked into the glazed eyes, the stricken stare.
Please don't cry… I'm much better, thank you.

The furry head nodded.

Shopping list

Get me a small sliced pan.
Make sure it's Brennan's white,
Not that wholemeal stuff.
Almost a full loaf in the bread bin.
Two large pans in the freezer.

Instead I buy her daffodils
spilling gold among the stale crumbs
on her oilclothed kitchen table.
She picks one up by its slender stem,
her eyes black holes,
grey mouth puckering in distress
at the sticky mess on her fingers.

Bringing pissybeds into the house!
You know what Mama says.
Her shaking hand falls
helpless by her side,
drops the offending flower.
Lips tremble like a child's.

I snip the weeping ends,
find an old Keller's marmalade jar
at the bottom of the kitchen press.
I need that jar.
Where's my change.
Where's my half-dozen eggs.

Upside Down Song

Little girl in the well
I see your wavering face,
Your eyes comma'd with tadpoles,
Weeds in your hair.

Little girl in the well
Three fields away from home,
Darkness fall so quickly
Should you be there alone?

Little girl in the well
Still waters are deep.
Beneath the blue of mirrored sky
Frogs spawn in slimy weeds.

Little girl in the well
Have you gone away?
Only the echoes answer
Have you gone away?

Inventory

Jim who wanders
Sarah who sits near the door
Jane who steals underwear
Tom who pees in other people's beds
Una who says
Hail Mary, Holy Mary
all day long

Red haired Rachel, fallen angel
starves herself to death
Joe never has a visitor,
rarely speaks
Trish has lost all her teeth
Silly Susan hides her pills, giggles
all day long

Veronica on a walking frame
Let me go home Let me go home
Mick and Joanie roam
hand in hand
Sit side by side in the dayroom
Josie piddles her pants, whimpers
all day long

All day long

Oasis

See that primrose!
My sister's voice was wry
unsentimental as always.
I peered at the puny leaves
the frail suggestions of yellow
nudging the concrete path under the clothes line.
It appeared the year he died
and every year since then.
She shrugged -
Seeds must have blown in from next door.
I've lost all interest in flowers.

But I noticed how carefully
she had mown
around the tufted edges
leaving this solitary exclamation
undisturbed.
And I wondered if she
who so rarely exclaimed
had found an outlet for her unshed tears
in this faint yearly blossoming.

Last Rites for Ber

I anoint your bruised head with a chrism of falling snow.

I anoint your swollen feet with foam from a Galtee stream.

I anoint your tired fingers with oil of woodbine and wild rose.

I anoint your white hair with gold dust from Russells' cornfield.

I anoint your closed eyes with cooling water from the well.

I place the whitest rose from the haggart in your still warm hands.

only

only a clay-black pit
only the lowered coffin
only a droning priest
only a thudding shovel

only a stifled laugh
only the muffled crying
only a smothered cough
only feet shuffling gravel

only a decade of beads
only a mumbling 'so sorry'
only the empty bed
only unthinkable to-morrow

RIP

so sorry dear
and did she suffer much
and for how long
and did she see a priest
and did the daughters cry

and dear who read in church
what priests were there
what did the daughters wear
how many wreaths
was it a big crowd
wish i'd been there

so sorry dear
didn't hear until too late
why pet you look quite pale
the house should fetch a bob or two
i called there when her
husband died
poor dear
didn't outlast him long

must be a family thing
didn't both your parents die
quite young
of course of course
you need to rest
i'll say goodbye
you *do* look white
so sorry dear

Now you will never know

Now you will never know
how Bertie fared at the polls.
Did Iran do as it was told.
When did the Yanks withdraw
from Iraq.
Did Saddam go free
or swing by the neck.

Now you will never feel again
the air become cold.
Branches bend under snow.
The year turn into a new birth.

Now you will never see
your youngest grandson
struggle to walk.
Amy graduate from baby-talk.
Donal's venture into Secondary School.

Now you will never hear again
Emma's hi gran rap on glass
flying hair flying feet.
Daniel's playstation uproar.
The signature tune of
Coronation Street.

Hold on a Minute

Yes? Hold on a minute while I turn the wireless down.
Your chemo starts next week.
I'll pray. Of course I will.

The only boy
he always get away with murder.
Our tortured knees
on stone-floored kitchen after tea,
Dada giving out the rosary.
His collar and tie on chair back in nightly ritual,
Prince tail-wagging at his feet.
Giggles behind rosaries
as starched collar circles Prince's neck.
But it was I was banished
to the candle-lit scullery.

Just a precaution?
You're ninety nine percent sure
 you're clear?

Small children with shared secrets.
Banned comics,
Beano, Dandy, Hotspur.
He always passed them on to me.
Our teacher-father surrounding us
with his own brand of culture
Pearse, Edgeworth, Scott, Mitchell's Jail Journal.

Thank you brother for Billy Bunter and fat Bessie-
our passport to the ordinary .

The Powers Within You?
 Positive Thinking?
No, I can't say I read any of these.

For days, weeks maybe
Mama packed his trunk for boarding school.
There was a flurry of strange talk.
Of nametapes, laundry bags, napkin rings.
The baby of the family
I envied all the fuss surrounding him
The trips to town to buy new clothes,
The sense of adventuring.

I do agree.
We've left it far too long.
You'll let me know if there's anything you need?

A stranger returned,
an inmate of another world
of scrums and tries and prefects
pillow fights in dorms.
And tea was in the parlour with Mama's Sunday cake
while my father listened proud-eyed to his only son.
And even Fr. Noonan came and talked grown-up talk to him.

The Way Home

Yes, he was a Bank Manager,
Chairman of Muintir na Tire,
Captain of the Golf Club -
Yes, he was all those things.
And a dozen more
charitable organisations
he helped or founded.

A tall woman in a long fur coat.
A man wearing glasses,
an air of importance.
Talking about someone
I didn't know -
denying me a reason for being there.

Outside, spring rain, a soft veil.
I wrap myself in it
as in a shroud.
A nasal voice drones.
People jostling,
umbrellas dripping.
The droning voice
dies away
in a clatter of feet, coughs,
car engines starting up.

Taking the familiar route
over the Slieve na Muc Hills
into the deep dark valley
of Aherlow,
passing peak after snowy peak
of the Galtees.

Below the snowline on Galtymore,
a small boy in knee pants,
fairisle pullover
and little black laced boots.

I turn the car into Russells' gateway
and for the first time
since my brother's death
allow myself to cry.

5

Tsunami

The circus is about to start
At first I am all heart
I play rock and sand
A melodeon crooning the wind.
Strike up the band

First I'm just a boy
skidding a flat stone across a pond
Now I somersault without a net
onto the beach
Tumble and leap

I lead the circus parade
Fat Lady bearded with weeds
Girl sawn in two in a glass tomb
Punch and Judy pummelled and bruised
I scent wet hair, wet flesh with greed

Now I'm a lion freed from his cage
A white horse mounting the waves
A clown's mouth all lips
A swallower of ships
A swallower of ships

I watch trustful houses sleeping
Hear them breathing
Watch them dreaming
Smother their screaming
Wash them cleanly

I was full of heart
To start with

Punchin' Judy

Never seem to get the knack of it
                          oh the knock of it
sock wham whack
one eye smiling
                          the other weeping
see my face in the policeman's boots
                          up down
                          down up

am I supposed to duck
is the policeman meant to save me
I know by heart every crack in the pavement
                          oh the knock of it
                          never- knowing knack of it
                          sock-wham laugh of it

Trick or Treat

When you laid me in the glass box
and strapped me down, I wore
only the flimsiest gold chiffon gown,
just the suggestion of a feather boa,
blue starred slippers on my feet.
I could hear the audience howl.
I was a goldfish in a goldfish bowl.

Your hand was warm at my waist
its rightful place, all my scars yours
your little mistakes, the sly barbs
of your trade. Then the moment
I feared. A flick of your fingers
and Hey presto! I disappeared.

I had watched you week after week
sharpening the teeth. The rasp and whine
as the saw bent and dipped.
Now it snarled my hair, pulled me down
stripped me, teased me
tossed me like a clown.

Did my understudy carry it off with flair.
When the panel slid back
did her golden hair shine like mine.
Did your caressing voice whisper
Divine
as the audience roared.

When you packed your saw
in its silver sheath with meticulous care.
And she wheeled your glass box
off the stage. When you pulled
a white rabbit out of a hat.
And pigeons flew out of nowhere.
Did you think you could conjure me back -
a feather, a slipper, a golden hair.

Betrayal

I didn't intend
to crack open
like an under done egg.

Too late
 to shout-
Sunny side up.

The whites
of my eyes
ran red.

The twelve at the table
soaked me up
with a piece of bread.

That should shut her up
for a while
someone said.

Old is

waking
to a door half open
a silence to be filled

 trying to remember
a dream the warm
touch   the shape of lips

 living on in a house
where young voices echo
though the air is still

an oak table
wooden grain laid bare
to every scrape and spill

the fear
of being buried alive
the daily struggle uphill

 a wax seal
instructions to ones survivors
the inanimate will

a silent platform
waiting room closed forever
rails rusted still

Crossing the blue line

Glass analyses the interior.
Nothing moves except
at the whim of light.

A magic lantern shows
a hedonistic dance
of bare buddleia on naked walls.
A joyful interplay.

From the heart of a glass
prism rainbowesque colours
hi-lite the hair of an old woman
sitting by the bookshelves.

They dance riotously on her open page.
Shimmer the wizened gold of her face.
Jewel her cheap ring with
rare opals rubies amethyst.

Glass analyses the interior.
Flames.
Dancing lights.
Outstretched shadows.

Beneath a standard lamp a head reads.
Lights from a passing car
bring alive a memory card
on a table bearing flowers.

The Last Cut

I drag out my mower for the last time.
Heavy going now as stiffening grass resists the blade.
Lumps of wet clay stick to the underside
and winter earth reveals a damping cold.

I shiver for the days of summer
when this cutting was a social thing and
neighbours urged each other on.
Constant whirrs, the humming drone.

Now only smoky chimney jets
the angelus bell
from the T.V. next door
tell that my neighbours are home.

My nails earth-black I turn the key
find the T.V. left on, the 6 o'clock news -
woman burned in flat, living alone -
I can do without that.

On the couch where I left it last night -
Life of Pi - only a few chapters left.
Finding the page.
Finding the page.

Afraid

I am afraid

When shop girls call me"pet" or "love"
when bank clerks say"take your time, dear"
when I forget my pin or worse

I am afraid

when I leave out the green bin on the purple day
when I check the door at night, check the door at night
when my husband calls me on the phone and says

I am afraid

when Saturday I see Friday's pills still in the box
when I dial the phone and the Tele comes on
when I come to roundabouts and roadblocks

I am afraid

when I can't find my glasses in their usual place
when I can't put a name to a face
when I go for a walk and its not the place

I am afraid

when people say I've told them before
when I know these are things I haven't said
when my husband calls me on the phone and says

I am afraid

And then

and then
there came the day
when I finally knew
I'd had enough of dwelling inside
time to venture
outside
the stories
in a million books
the walking stick
gathering dust
behind my bookshelves
fitted snugly
in my grasp

and so I went
where I had no right to go
they said
when they warned me
of what lay ahead
the naked stones
on the hill path
are flecked with blood
your shoes are too thin
your clumsy feet will slip
your old eyes
not fine-tuned enough
to recognise

the subtle twists and turns
that would lead you on
to higher ground

I smile
see them frown
I have no doubts
my walking stick fits
like a glove
I will be happy
if I can get
even one tenth of the way
I can take my time
see
that white light
covering the ridge
can it be snow

The Great Escape

Old Kate has built a snowman in her drive.
Timmy's new van has not been moved for days.
Yesterday saw the postman take a dive.
I 'll chance my luck no matter what they say.

Timmy's new van has not been moved for days.
I'm tired of Countdown. Eggheads leaves me cold.
I'll chance my luck no matter what they say.
No, no I'm not too helpless or too old.

I'm tired of Countdown. Eggheads leaves me cold.
I don my warmest coat, gloves, fur lined boots.
No, no I'm not too helpless or too old.
In fact I'm fearless and don't give a hoot.

I don my warmest coat, gloves, fur lined boots.
Stick my nose out, the air should make me cringe.
In fact I'm fearless and don't give a hoot.
I grit my teeth step out and do not whinge.

Stick my nose out, the air should make me cringe.
Yesterday saw the postman take a dive.
I grit my teeth step out and do not whinge.
Old Kate has built a snowman in her drive.

The Green Wheelbarrow
for Mary

There was an old woman named Mrs. O'Marrow
Who drove her grass cuttings
round in a barrow.
Grass cuttings to sell.
Grass cuttings to sell.
Biodegradable
Decompose well
by bacterial means.
Hedge cuttings as well.

Nobody heeded poor Mrs. O'Marrow.
She took her grass cuttings
out of the barrow.
Stuffed them in to a purple sack.
It weighed a ton
but she didn't slack.
Dragged her burden outside the fence
to be collected by the garbage men.

But the bag remained outside the fence.
Too heavy they said.
It was an offence.
Fifteen kilos was too much to swallow.
So what did she do old Mrs. O'Marrow?
She put the grass cuttings
back in the barrow.
A garden feature she told her friends.

She stopped cutting grass, laid off
topping hedges.
But people still grumbled
said the growth was offensive.
Could she find any use
for that fine big barrow?
Don't tempt me, don't tempt me
Said Mrs. O'Marrow.

The Man in the Brown Suit
for Margaret

My front door bell isn't working.
Discovered it just now.
Two o'clock
On a wet and windy Sunday afternoon.
Had just switched off Murder She Wrote.
Nothing till Miss Marple at 3.45.

Then through my front window I saw
A suited stranger walk out my drive.
 I ducked - but too late.
A bang at the door -
A card thrust in my face.
Mr. FIXIT- no job too big or small.

Your bell isn't working, Ma'am.
He wasn't very tall.
A shabby brown suit.
Unremarkable I suppose you'd say.
Really, I sneered.
It worked perfectly an hour ago.
Then slammed the door in his face.

But when I tried it -
 Not a beep!
Would you believe it.
Just like that!
After 31 years.
Makes you wonder.

The Cat who Comes
for Phyllis

The cat who comes is beautiful.
Sinuous.
Elusive.
We are not on first name terms.
I call her 'cat'.
She brushes her perfect head
against my knee.
Her sea green eyes
reflect nothing.
I like that.

No, she is not the cat
visits my friend's neighbour
at the back.
No, not that starved created
they describe
who laps up saucers of milk,
then disappears.
My visitor drinks water only.
Daintily nibbles tuna chunks
from her new dish.
I happen to be partial to fish.

Sometimes she jumps on my lap
when I sit on the deckchair
in the rare sunshine.
She doesn't press close.
Leaves me room
to read,
do my crossword,
watch the buddliea come alive,
the cotoneasters swarm with bees.

She goes as secretively as she comes.
Sometimes I catch sight
of the white tip of her tail
disappearing behind the pampas grass.
Or a hint of brown
among the long green spikes.
I know she'll be back.
Maybe to-morrow.
Maybe next week.
I like that.

Beloved

after Toni Morrison

You came to me all ragged and forlorn.
I took you in and loved you as my child.
Knew nothing of your past. Where you were born.
Your coat was torn your lovely green eyes wild.

I loved. Some say I cosseted and spoiled.
You went your way. Breakfasted at dawn.
Then out the door you sped wayward child.
You came to me all ragged and forlorn.

Your disappearing acts I could have borne.
One morning when I scolded you were riled.
My undefended face by sharp nails torn.
I took you in and loved you as my child.

Some say you ventured from the other side.
When you needed me you came. Now I am torn.
A distant memory of a mind gone wild.
Knew nothing of your past. Where you were born.

But when I look at you your green eyes warn
Remember jagged skin hands blood-soiled
I gave you milk. Did not want you harmed.
Your coat was torn your lovely green eyes wild.

Sometimes you seem so sweet so meek and mild.
Like a mewling kitten that's just been born.
I want to kiss and hug you like a child.
To love you and to hold you in my arms.

You came to me.

An Teampall Geal

Easter morning. Early.
A sloping hill field.
Three priests white-robed
against the wall of a ruined church.

Waking sun spilling
over long line of Kerry hills
into a paschal fire
blazing in the furze.

Footsteps and voices.
Faces coming out of the mist
of shadowy little fields
glad with sheep.

Shavasana

for Anne

curtains drawn
fire shifts slightly
quick flame
silver frames my daughters
on the mantel shelf

door shut
on the giant face
of the clock in the hall

footsteps a long way off
disappear like clouds
my closed book
a silent mouth

eyes shut
in out in out
I breathe

Surya Namaskara
for Deirdre

when the time comes
space without a here or there
a longed-for silence
the painter slits the sky

an anchored boat is washed
in a sea of light
overpainting shadows
fore and aft

nothing moves except the light
gold brush-strokes on the sails -
uptilted sunflower

Against The Tide
(after a Seminole chant for the dying)

Come back
Before you get to the top of the Galtees
Come back
Before you get to the lower lake
Come back
Before you get to Glencushabinna
Come back
Before you get to Aherlow Glen
Come back
Before you get to the crossroads
Come back
Before you get to the well field
Come back
Before you get to the haggart
Come back
Before you get to the half-door
Come back
Before you get to the open fire
Come back
Before you get to the middle of the ladder
leading to your bed in the loft